WHO CAN?

Florence Parry Heide
Sylvia Worth Van Clief

Carl B. Smith
Ronald Wardhaugh

Macmillan Publishing Co., Inc.
New York

Collier Macmillan Publishers
London

SERIES **r**

Macmillan Reading

ACKNOWLEDGMENTS

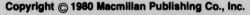

Illustrations: Ray Cruz, pp. 2-3; Jerry Smath, pp. 14-21; Les Grey, pp. 22-29; Lowren West, pp. 30-41, 62-63; Ted Shroder, pp. 42-49; Stan Zagorsky, pp. 50-59; Olivia Cole, pp. 60-61. **Photographs:** David Attie, pp. 4-13. **Cover Design:** AKM Associates

Parts of this work were published in SERIES Γ: The New Macmillan Reading Program.

Macmillan Publishing Co., Inc.
866 Third Avenue, New York, New York 10022
Collier Macmillan Canada, Ltd.

Printed in the United States of America
ISBN 0-02-128250-1
9876543

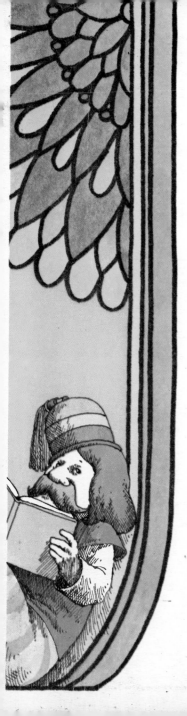

Contents

4

I Can

5

I can jump.

Can you jump, too?

7

I can ride.

Can you ride, too?

9

I can run.

Can you run, too?

I can read.

Can you read, too?

You Can, Too

You can't run.

You can run.
But you can't jump.

You can run and jump.
But you can't ride.

You can run
and jump
and ride.
But you can't fish.

19

You can run
and jump
and ride.

And you can fish!

21

Dogs

23

I like little dogs.
Little dogs sit.

I like big dogs.
Big dogs jump.

Little dogs jump, too.
Jump, little dogs, jump!

Down, little dogs, down!

26

Sit, little dogs, sit!

Down, big dogs, down!

I like little dogs.

The Little Man and

the Big Man

The little man jumps.

He likes to jump.

He likes to jump.

So he jumps.

The big man says,
"I can't jump.
But I can sit.
I like to sit.
So I sit."

The little man runs.
He likes to run.
He likes to run.
So he runs.

34

The big man says,
"I can't jump.
And I can't run.

But I can sit.
I like to sit.
So I sit."

The little man rides.
He likes to ride.
He likes to ride.
So he rides.

The big man says,
"I can't jump.
I can't run.
And I can't ride.

But I can sit.
I like to sit.
So I sit."

The little man says,
"I can jump.
And I can run.
But I can't ride."

The little man
and the big man
sit and sit
and sit.

39

I Like

Boys:

I like to walk.

I like to run.

Girls:

I like to jump.

I like to ride.

Boys and girls:

I like to sit and read.

Boys:

I like to go up.
I like to go down.

Girls:

I like to jump in.
I like to jump out.

Girls:

I like fish.
I like dogs.

Boys and girls:

I like boys.
I like girls.
And I like you.

43

Bob likes to fish.
Why?
Why does Bob like to fish?

Bob likes fish.
That is why
he likes to fish.

Bob likes little fish
and big fish.

Bob likes to sit and fish.

Bob says,
"I like fish.
I like to sit
and fish."

The fish go to Bob.
The fish like Bob.
And that is why
Bob likes to fish.

That Man

Part One
Who Is That Man?

Why does he walk
and walk and walk?

Why does he walk
up and down?

Why does that man run?
Why does he run
into the house?
Why does he run
out of the house?

Why does that man jump?
Why does he jump
into the car?
Why does he jump
out of the car?

Part Two
Why? Why?

Why does that man look?

Why does he look up the hill?

Why does he look

down the hill?

Why does he look
into the house?
Why does he look
out of the house?

Why does he walk and walk?
Why does he run and run?
Why does he jump and jump?
Why does he look and look?
Why does he call and call?

The man calls a dog.
The dog runs to the man.
The man and the dog
go to the house.

59

Why?

Why does grass grow up,
    not down?
Why does a smile look better
    than a frown?

How does a seed know
    what to be?
And why are you **you**
    instead of me?

A Word Game

The girl says car.
The boy says ....

    The girl says run.
    The boy says ....

The girl says look.
The boy says ....

    The girl says jump.
    The boy says ....

The boy says ride.
The girl says ....

The boy says hill.
The girl says ....

The boy says fish.
The girl says ....

The boy says house.
The girl says ....

WORD LIST

5. I	23. dogs	to	out	55. car
can	24. like	so	42. Bob	56. two
6. jump	little	33. says	44. why	look
7. you	sit	34. runs	does	hill
too	25. big	36. rides	45. that	58. call
8. ride	26. down	40. boys	is	59. *calls*
10. run	30. the	girls	52. part	a
12. read	man	walk	one	*dog*
16. can't	32. *jumps*	41. go	who	62. word
17. but	he	up	54. into	game
18. and	*likes*	in	house	*girl*
19. fish			of	*boy*

To the Teacher: The words listed beside the page numbers above are found in *Who Can?* Level 4 of SERIES r. The underlined words were introduced in Level 3. The children should be able to use previously taught skills to identify the italicized words independently.

64